FIDUCIWHO?

FIDUCIWHO?
What a Real Fiduciary Will Tell You about How to Protect, Grow, Enjoy, and
Transfer Your Wealth

ISBN (paperback): 978-1-956220-81-0
ISBN (hardback): 978-1-956220-95-7

Expert Press
www.ExpertPress.net

Editing by Ty Hager
Copyediting by Wendy Lukasiewicz
Proofreading by Geena Barrett

Text design and composition by Emily Fritz
Cover design by Casey Fritz

FIDUCIWHO?

WHAT A REAL FIDUCIARY WILL TELL YOU ABOUT HOW TO PROTECT, GROW, ENJOY, AND TRANSFER YOUR WEALTH

LEONARD P. RASKIN

MSFS, CFP™, CHFC, CLU, CAP, CASL, AEP

This book is dedicated to my wife of thirty years, Kathy, for all her love and support, and to my son, Matthew, who can't believe I wrote anything longer than an email.

Read More from a Real Fiduciary at RaskinGlobal.com

Contents

Introduction

"What's going on in your world?"

This is how every journey with my clients begins. I ask the question because I want to know who you are, not just how much you want to invest. I want to know your hopes and dreams, not just financially but personally. I want to know not just how you see your future but how you see your family's future.

My name is Leonard Raskin. For over thirty-six years I've helped individuals and families find security and peace of mind. How? By helping them understand that happiness doesn't come from making the right investments at the right time; happiness comes from looking at the "big picture" and implementing lifelong strategies based on their unique situation and goals. Long term. Over generations.

I don't call myself a "financial advisor," although I advise my clients about their finances. I don't call myself a "retirement planner," although I help my clients plan for retirement. I don't call myself an "estate planner," although I help my clients there too. With a master's degree in financial services and multiple professional certifications in financial planning, insurance, philanthropy, and estate planning, I've developed a radically different approach to wealth management.

I don't put on my financial advisor or retirement planner or estate planner hats only when they're needed. I wear these hats all the time because they're all part of your financial big picture. To use another analogy, if all you have in your toolbox is a hammer, everything is going to be a nail. If your advisor makes a living selling annuities, then an annuity is going to be the solution to your financial goals. If your advisor is strictly an investment advisor, then investments will be your solution.

I've got a much bigger toolbox.

Thousands of books have been written about financial planning. Many, if not most, of these books are trying to sell you on a particular strategy or financial product. That's not this book.

I've always said that there are three distinct types of knowledge: what you know you know, what you know you don't know, and what you don't know you don't know. There's an old quote—often attributed to Mark Twain, but no one really knows for sure where it came from—that takes this concept a step farther: "It ain't what you don't know that gets you into trouble. It's what you know for sure that just ain't so." One of my primary goals with this book is to show you, if you'll pardon the pun, "where the twain shall meet." There may be information here that you know you already know. There will be much that you know you didn't know. There will be plenty that you didn't know you didn't know. And I suspect there will be lots that you knew for sure that "just ain't so."

Along the way, we're going to talk about four key objectives to successful generational wealth management: protecting, growing, *enjoying*, and transferring. You'll soon understand why I italicized "enjoying." (Hint: If you're not enjoying your wealth, nothing else matters.) You'll learn that these objectives aren't sequential but concurrent—that they're all intertwined threads running through the same fabric of your financial life. They're different trains running on parallel tracks, heading to the same station. They all need to be on the right track.

I'll teach you, in the same straightforward manner I teach all my clients, to break through the clutter of an immensely complex financial landscape. You will better understand not only the "how to" of these four objectives but, more importantly, the "what for?"

I'll also show you why planning (whether it's financial planning, retirement planning, or estate planning) can be a fool's errand when left to the devices of so many who call themselves "planners."

As my mother says, "Man plans, God laughs." Traditional planning tends to be geared not toward the client but toward the one creating (and usually selling) the plan. This approach ignores the ever-changing variables on a multitude of fronts, all those "what-ifs" lying in wait to ruin any plan: What if I get sued? What if I get sick or become disabled? What if the market crashes or interest rates soar? What if I die too soon (or live too long)? What if the government tries to take more of my stuff?

If your plan fails to take these questions into consideration, it's not really a plan.

Over the years, I've educated thousands of clients (and their families) on the principles and concepts contained in this book. I'll relate some of their stories. I'll show you why it's important to buck the harmful tradition of "not talking about money" with family members, and why open and honest communication about financial matters, well, matters.

Your goals—for yourself and your family—are my goals. It's my job to help you get there sooner and safer than you thought possible. Often, I'm able to help you see that you're selling yourself short—that the goals you set aren't just achievable but that you can do more.

You need a professional. I tell my clients all the time, "If you think hiring a pro is expensive, you should try hiring an amateur. Or try doing it yourself."

Now that's expensive.

Relying on video talking heads or insurance salespeople or stockbrokers can be catastrophic to your financial well-being.

SECTION I
Protect Your Wealth
Answering the "What-Ifs"

In ancient times (or if you're feeling archaic, days of yore), kings had to secure their land before they could assemble armies to conquer new lands.

So they built moats around their castles. And they built walls.

In the twenty-first century, your "castle" is more than your home—it's your kingdom. It's your life. It's your health. It's your wealth. And it's your and your family's future.

It must be protected.

In order to fully secure our own castles and kingdoms, we have to understand—and be prepared to counter—all the worst-case scenarios. All those "what-ifs."

In the next few chapters, we're going to talk about those what-ifs and how (and why) it takes sound and multilayered wealth management to thwart the progress and pain of any what-if that may come your way.

If I had to hazard a guess, I'd estimate that about 99 percent of advisors or self-professed fiduciaries focus their efforts on only a few of these what-ifs. The ones that can be remedied by the limited tools in their toolbox. It's not that they don't care about the other what-ifs—it's that they don't know how to address them, and they don't get paid to address them.

Not long ago I was at a conference in Florida attended by five hundred or so other registered fiduciaries. While most of my fellow attendees called themselves (and were registered as) fiduciaries, they were actually investment advisors. Taken as a whole, they successfully managed around $10 billion in wealth for their clients. They're good at what they do. Their clients make money and—as these folks get paid a percentage of the assets they manage—they're making money as well.

But investment advisors are all about growth. The what-ifs they take into account are limited to those that can be fixed with the tools in their toolbox. They're (hopefully) good at anticipating fluctuations in markets and interest rates and implementing strategies to counter those. They have the tools, and they know how to use them.

But what about all those other what-ifs? I'm willing to bet that the majority of their clients—if faced with a major lawsuit, catastrophic illness, or any other what-ifs not included in this investment company's particular toolbox—could end up devastated.

You know who wouldn't face such devastation?

Our clients.

1
WHAT IF I GET SUED?

America is a litigious nation. If you get into a car accident and it was your fault? You're going to get sued. If you own a brick-and-mortar business and a customer slips on a spill and hurts their hip? You're going to get sued. Same thing if you produce a product that causes damage, injury, or worse. If you own a medical practice, when it comes to lawsuits, the designation "MD" can mean "more dollars," and such perils are always just around the corner.

The list goes on and on. Lawsuits can ruin you. Indeed, they have ruined many. So how can a comprehensive wealth management strategy not include protection against such a catastrophic scenario?

Short answer: It can't.

That brings us to insurance and asset titling. I bet you saw where this was headed.

As with many of the what-ifs we'll be discussing in this section, insurance—in multiple forms—is going to play a role in the solution. The problem is that most financial advisors are only going to address the risks their particular tools are able to fix. It is their fiduciary duty to put the best interests of the client first, but that scope is usually limited to how those interests can be addressed by the financial products they have to sell. They might be so-called experts on investments but not even ask you about the insurance on your car.

That's just not in their toolbox.

THE DIRTY LITTLE SECRET ABOUT THE INSURANCE INDUSTRY

We all know that the insurance companies want you to buy their products. That's why there are policies that cover everything from your cell phone to your life. But here's what they don't tell you:

The insurance industry doesn't want you to have *too much* coverage.

This is, of course, in stark contrast to the foundation of capitalism. For most manufacturers of products and providers of services, there's no such thing as "too much." Even the makers of alcohol and tobacco products—despite their government-mandated warnings to the contrary—want you to drink and smoke. A lot.

Not insurance companies. Yes, they want everyone to be covered. What they don't want is for everyone to be covered enough. Their entire business model, with all its statistical and actuarial data, relies on having the highest number of customers with the least amount of coverage. Insurance agents are compensated based on the amount of premiums collected, but there are some insurance agents whose compensation is *reduced* by the total amount of claims paid out. More coverage means higher premiums coming in to the insurance company, but it also means potentially higher claims payouts to the insureds.

Insurance companies don't like that.

Take the insurance you have on your vehicles, for example. Pretty much every state requires you to have a set amount of liability coverage for property damage and bodily injury, and approximately a third of people driving around have this minimum coverage. A few states also require that you have personal injury protection (PIP), which covers the cost of your passengers' and your injuries, or uninsured/ underinsured motorist (UM/UIM) coverage, or both. In my home state of Maryland, you're required to have $30,000 bodily injury coverage for each of up to two occupants of the other vehicle (so a maximum of $60,000) and $15,000 for property damage. You also have to have that same amount of UM/UIM coverage, with an additional $2,500 in PIP.

You may be, according to your auto insurance agent, "fully covered" and have—in addition to what's legally required—things like comprehensive, collision, and medical payment coverage (along with the UM/UIM and PIP, if those aren't legally required in your state). But have you seen the costs of medical treatment and cars lately? If you're at fault in a serious accident, these damages can easily exceed your coverage. Often, by a lot. If you've accumulated some wealth, own a home, and have income, the attorneys will come for that.

What if you're not at fault and the other driver doesn't have enough insurance to pay for your damages? What if they don't have additional assets? This could easily be a threat to your total life's wealth creation as well.

THERE'S NO SUCH THING AS "TOO MUCH" COVERAGE

A few years ago, a client called me over the Christmas break. He and his wife, along with their two young daughters, were in their SUV, driving on a two-lane road in Texas, when a woman in another car crossed into their lane and hit them head-on. Thankfully, all survived, but one of the daughters suffered two broken legs.

The other driver had the minimum coverage in Texas, which at the time was $20,000 for bodily injury. My client called me in a panic. Beyond the stress of worrying over his daughter's recovery, he also knew that $20,000 wasn't going to make a dent in the costs for surgery, rehabilitation, and any unknown long-term consequences of her injuries. He wanted to know what additional coverage he had. It just so happened that, per my advice, they had UM/UIM coverage of up to

WHAT IF I GET SUED?

$2.5 million. Most don't have anywhere near that amount of coverage (and most insurance agents will tell you it's too much), but I'm a firm believer that you can't be overinsured.

My client didn't end up needing that insurance. Turns out the woman who hit his SUV was delivering a pizza for Pizza Hut. With the help of an attorney in Texas (who was also stunned by the amount of insurance coverage my client had), he ended up getting a settlement for about three-quarters of a million bucks.

But what if the other driver hadn't been driving for Pizza Hut? What if my clients hadn't had that additional coverage? What if my clients had been at fault? All these what-ifs, these convergences of almost-unimaginable scenarios, can add up to disaster, and you have to be protected.

A SMALL PRICE TO PAY

Most people who don't have the extra insurance protection needed to cover those what-ifs think it's too expensive. It isn't—especially when you think about the cost of not having it.

I was on a Zoom call recently with a couple who was considering hiring me. He owns a business on which he has $1 million in liability insurance. They have $250,000 in liability insurance for their home and the same for their car.

I asked them if they had insurance on their cell phones. They nodded, but the question seemed to surprise them.

"And what do you pay for yours?" I asked the husband.

"About ten bucks a month, I think."

"So one hundred and twenty dollars per year," I said (because I'm quick with math that way).

I told them that for that same amount, they could likely have an additional $1 million liability insurance on their vehicle. That would protect their assets and income from a lawsuit if an accident were their fault, and it would protect them against damages from an accident with an at-fault but uninsured/underinsured motorist.

They're now clients.

There are many types of lawsuits that don't involve car accidents, and there are types of insurance to protect against those too. A doctor client of mine called me recently,overcome with fear because one of his colleagues was being sued. He thought he might be next.

"What do I do?" he implored me.

He seemed a little put off when I chuckled and said, "You don't have to do a thing."

"What are you talking about?" he cried. "My friend's about to lose it all."

I assured him that—while I certainly felt for his colleague—he didn't have anything whatsoever to worry about.

"You're covered," I said.

Successful wealth management must address anything and everything that threatens what you have now or can get in the way of future earnings. Insurance—*adequate* insurance—can be a powerful and crucial part of your arsenal.

2

WHAT IF I GET SICK OR
BECOME DISABLED?

Protecting your castle involves more than safeguarding it from risks outside the walls. You have to be vigilant to the dangers from within—you have to protect your assets and income from the threats posed by illness and disability.

I'm sure you've heard that there's insurance for that.

If you're a US citizen walking around without at least a basic health insurance plan . . . shame on you. Sorry to scold, but the risks are too great, and the cost—while in many cases more than it should be—still pales in comparison to the cost of not having insurance when you need it.

I could go on and on about all the flaws in America's health care industry and how I think it could be better. Much better. I could probably fill another entire book. But this book isn't about that.

For the purposes of this chapter, we're going to assume that, like most Americans, you have some kind of health insurance. Whether it's through Medicare or private insurance through your employer or the Affordable Care Act, if you or a member of your family gets sick, has an accident, or needs surgery, your medical costs are covered. Rather, we're going to talk about how (and why) protecting yourself from all the financial risks that go far beyond medical treatment will factor into your wealth management strategy.

This is something else most financial advisors and fiduciaries won't pay much attention to.

CALCULATING THE COST

Unless you're already retired (or nearing retirement), your greatest asset isn't your home. It isn't your stock portfolio. The greatest asset you own as a revenue-producing body moving through time is your ability to generate income.

Full stop. Your greatest treasure is your treasure-making potential.

Many people, like the thirty-five-year-old prospective client I visited last week, drastically underestimate what this number might be.

If this client wants to retire at age sixty-five, he has thirty years of earnings ahead of him. He currently makes in the ballpark of $85,000 per year. Even if his income doesn't increase a dime over the next thirty years, he has around $2.5 million in total gross income on his horizon. He's a pretty sharp guy, so most likely we're talking about significantly more than that. With a 3 percent raise per year, his total income will exceed $4 million.

If he becomes disabled in an accident, there's a chance he might be able to get fair compensation in a settlement. But what if he has a stroke or a heart attack and is suddenly no longer able to work? What if he's never able to work again?

Unless he's protected, that $2.5 million or $4 million or however-many millions of dollars of potential earnings is going to fall to zero. Forever beyond his horizon.

It's not only that future income that vanishes. It's going to be replaced by more expenses, many (or most) of which likely won't be covered under your health plan. What if you need in-home nursing care? What if, God forbid, you have to go to a nursing home? You could easily be looking at hundreds of thousands of dollars (or much, much more) in out-of-pocket costs throughout the remainder of your life.

It's easy, and convenient, to tell ourselves that these scenarios are among those what-ifs that aren't going to happen to us. That's our cognitive bias talking. Nobody wants to envision the worst. We have a tendency to think that if we picture it happening—and especially if we plan for it—we're going to jinx ourselves.

That's silly. The reality is that all these things are possible, and responsible and successful wealth management dictates that they not be what-ifs we ignore. There are thousands of tragic examples of people who never thought such things could ever happen to them, only to lose everything they owned when they did happen.

When you're in the prime earning phase of your life, it's easy to tell yourself that it makes more economic sense to roll the dice. That there's a better chance you'll be struck by lightning than that you'll become permanently disabled or suffer a stroke and have to be put in a nursing home. That the money spent on what is surely excessive insurance is better left to grow in the marketplace until a few years down the road, when the odds against a serious health incident aren't so remote.

My job is to make sure that—if lightning does strike—you're covered. To show you how the peace of mind that comes with such security adds to your enjoyment of life, and how whatever small sacrifices made to your current growth strategy pale in comparison to the consequences of ignoring the well-proven fact that lightning does, indeed, strike. And how small sacrifices now can easily lead to more growth down the line.

TYPES OF PROTECTION

There are a number of ways you can keep yourself safe from lightning strikes. The following are a few of the more common protections.

DISABILITY INCOME INSURANCE

As a rule of thumb, disability income insurance usually costs 1–3 percent of your annual wages and will cover from 50–80 percent of those wages to retirement. Because (as I've stated) you can't be over insured, I recommend you have the most coverage you can get. If you're still fairly young, extending the waiting period will lower your rates.

LONG-TERM CARE INSURANCE

Long-term care insurance covers things like in-home nursing care, assisted living facilities, and nursing homes. It's a bit pricier than most disability insurance, partly because the costs of the services themselves are exorbitant. According to Consumer Affairs in 2022, the average American spent $140,000 out-of-pocket on this type of care.[1] With that in mind, insurance isn't cost-prohibitive—especially if you get it while you're in your fifties (or even younger).

LIFE INSURANCE AND ANNUITY RIDERS

Life insurance and annuity riders offer ways to cover both disability and long-term care, with tax benefits and even growth potential not available with traditional disability and long-term care coverage. We'll talk (a lot) more about life insurance (including annuities) in the next chapter.

---

1   Sandy Baker, "What is the cost of in-home care?", ConsumerAffairs.com, March 23, 2022. https://www.consumeraffairs.com/health/in-home-care-cost.html.

I mentioned in the introduction that the key elements of successful wealth management—protect, grow, enjoy, and transfer—are like trains on parallel tracks. It may seem like having a plan for all these what-ifs benefits the protect train to the detriment of the grow and enjoy trains. The thing is, all four trains are heading to the same station, and there are going to be plenty of twists and turns (and maybe even some blocked tunnels and washed-out bridges) along the way.

A single major health event, with no guardrails in place, can derail them all.

3

What If I Die Too Soon (or Live Too Long)?

More on Life Insurance

I don't want to be the bearer of bad news. I don't want to rain on your parade, be a Gloomy Gus, or bum you out.

But you're going to die.

All living inhabitants of this planet have two things in common: We're all born and, at some point, we all die. For us humans, I like to call this sad and inescapable truth "when your will matures." It sounds better than "when you die," but it means the same thing.

We'll cover wills more when we get into the "transfer" section of the book. This chapter is all about life insurance: some of the different types of life insurance, the role it plays in protecting your castle (your wealth), and how having the right coverage can prolong your life.

Life insurance can be a lifesaver.

WHAT YOU NEED TO KNOW

Life insurance can seem complex. Oftentimes, it is complex. This chapter won't make you an expert on the subject, but it will show you how life insurance can be an integral part of your overall wealth management strategy and why having an expert in your corner is so important.

No one wants to leave their family in a financial crisis upon their passing. Of course not. We want to protect them from that. For most people, a life insurance policy will be their greatest transference of wealth when that inevitable day comes. When their will matures. That's why you'll often hear people say things like "I'm worth more dead than alive."

That's a silly statement that people usually make because they've heard it before without thinking it through. Yes, it's true that if you have even one dollar of life insurance coverage, you're worth more dead than alive. But those are just numbers. They don't take into consideration a lifetime of earning potential. And they don't factor in your value as a human being to those who love you.

So everyone is and isn't "worth more dead than alive." But I digress.

Life insurance comes in all shapes and sizes. There's *term, whole, universal,* and *variable.* There are policies that are hybrids of each of these. But every life insurance policy is either going to be *term life* or *permanent life.* The former, term life, is what the name implies: It covers you for a *term,* or a specific period of time. Some policies are good for ten years. Some fifteen. Some are good for twenty or even thirty years. Then your coverage *term*inates.

Term life is what most people have, mainly because they think it's the cheapest and the easiest to understand. But term life comes with great risk: It builds no cash value whatsoever, and if you outlive the term of the policy (which, frankly, is going to be your goal), you're out of luck. Even worse, your family's out of luck. Think about it. How would you like to tell your family, "Good news! I lived longer than the term of my life insurance policy. I'm still here, just without life insurance." All that hard-earned money you've spent to protect your loved ones from the worst will be gone. To add insult to injury, you may—depending on your age and health when your term life policy expires—find it difficult (if not impossible) to get another. If you are able to get one, it will almost certainly be more expensive. Possibly by a lot.

Creating a successful wealth management plan using term life insurance as part of the strategy is like trying to coach a football team in a game without a set play clock—one in which the referee could blow the final whistle at any moment, without notice. With term life, the ref could blow that whistle while your team is losing.

Permanent life insurance is different. The name is somewhat misleading. The only thing permanent in life is a lack of permanence. One of the most common types of permanent life insurance (and one with a far more accurate name) is *whole life insurance.* Because, you guessed it, it covers you for your whole life. These policies are going to have higher premiums but offer so many benefits that term life doesn't have that it's well worth it.

For starters, whole life policies build up cash value. It's as if a portion of your premiums are paid into a savings account that accrues over time. Once earned, this cash value can never go down. This built-up cash value can be used as collateral, enabling you to borrow against the account. This can be done via a direct loan from the insurance company or through an outside lender. You can even, at some point, use this cash value to provide income in retirement. Some of these policies even have the option of adding riders for things like long-term care, chronic or critical illnesses, or even a *waiver of premium* (which means you get to keep your insurance if your health or an accident prevents you from being able to pay your premium). The insurance company pays the premium for you, which continues to increase your cash value as if you were paying the policy yourself.

In all my years of giving financial advice, I've seen thousands of different investment vehicles—not a single other one has a waiver of premium provision.

A wealth management strategy using permanent life insurance is still like playing a football game where the final whistle could blow at any time—you just know that all your players are going to be good for the long haul. Tireless. For your whole life.

HOW MUCH LIFE INSURANCE DO I NEED?

As I mentioned earlier the insurance companies don't want you to have the amount of coverage you may actually need. This is true throughout the industry, whether you're protecting yourself from car accidents and health crises or protecting your family after you're gone.

Most life insurance agents, financial advisors, and insurance companies will recommend you purchase protection equal to five to ten times the amount of your annual income (if that). Most people get coverage through work equal to one to two times their earnings and think they have enough. Unless you're already quite old, that's a ridiculously low amount. What if you're in your forties? You could easily have a quarter-century or more of earning potential. Buying too little life insurance is like telling your family that they'll be okay—for a little while. After that? Too bad, so sad.

Rather (and this is a good rule of thumb, without getting too mathematically complex), you should buy life insurance equal to your gross annual income for the number of years until you turn sixty-five. If you're thirty-five and make $100,000 a year, you should buy a $3 million policy. If you're forty-five, you should have a $2 million policy. It may cost you an extra $1,000 every year, but that's less than the cost of your daily Starbucks.

It's worth it.

The better question to ask is "How much life insurance do I *want?*"

LIFE INSURANCE FOR THE LIVING

Survey after survey has shown that one of Americans' greatest fears is running out of money before they run out of life. Alleviating this fear is at the core of successful wealth management.

I told you about the cash value certain permanent life policies offer and how this can be used in time to receive loans to live on. Yes, I said a loan to *live on*. If you've ever heard of a reverse mortgage, you'll understand that borrowing money for cash flow in retirement and paying this loan off at your death can be a great financial strategy. Your life insurance can do the same.

Additionally, there are life insurance products that can be used to provide you with a regular income until the day your will matures and still pass along benefits to your survivors.

These are called *annuities*.

You've probably heard or read a lot of nasty things about annuities—mainly from those whose best interests are served if you believe those things. But annuities are life insurance products that are backed by the full financial strength of the insurance company issuing them, and they've been around since the days of the Roman Empire. Benjamin Franklin bought them. So did Babe Ruth. (Franklin's $4,500 annuities had, by 1990, reaped over $6 million for the cities of Boston and Philadelphia; Ruth's annuity meant that—after his will matured—his widow was financially secure for the rest of her life.)

At their core, annuities are a way to purchase a guaranteed future income. For the most part, they're much more like Social Security than "playing the market." They can be purchased in one lump sum or with monthly premiums, and there are riders available to cover death benefits, long-term care, and even protection against inflation. There are even annuities that offer guaranteed growth with no risk of loss. *Zero.*

Ignore the naysayers. Annuities can be a powerful tool in your wealth management toolbox.

LESS STRESS EQUALS A LONGER LIFE

We all know that stress is a killer. It can lead to anxiety and depression. It can lead to high blood pressure, which leads to heart attacks and strokes. It can make your hair fall out (although that's rarely life-threatening). Worrying about finances and protecting your family against worst-case scenarios can be a major source of such stress.

That's one more reason proper wealth management is so important. Appropriate life insurance and income-producing annuities offer protection that can help reduce stress and enhance longevity.

4

WHAT IF THE
MARKET CRASHES?

Let me start by saying this: Whether a market crash even matters to you will be entirely dependent on your financial life cycle.

We hear a lot about "market volatility" these days. I laugh when one of these financial talking heads on TV or YouTube says, "We're looking at an extremely volatile trading environment" or "There are more sellers than buyers today." (I've heard both of these statements.)

Guess what? Wall Street has always been volatile. Fluctuations in the stock market (aka, its volatility) are kind of the point. That's how people make money in the market. That's also how they lose money.

And guess what else? There are never *ever* more sellers than buyers. It's a mathematical impossibility—for every share of stock that is sold, there is a buyer; for every share of stock that is bought, there is a seller. Fluctuations in the market are nothing more than a reflection of whether it's the sellers or the buyers who are getting the better deal.

Trading on Wall Street is a bit more complicated than that, but not necessarily as complex as the "experts" would have you believe.

When most investors think of volatility, they ignore the market going up; they're worried about (and keenly aware of) it going down. And for those who have a considerable amount of their wealth invested in their stock portfolio, they're worried about a crash.

A CRASH COURSE ON CRASHES

Crashes—generally defined in the financial world as abrupt, unexpected, and dramatic drops in the stock market—are fairly rare and pretty famous. There was the big one, the Great Crash, in 1929 that ushered in the Great Depression. The Dow Jones (the sole market index of the time) dropped about 25 percent over two days and had, within three years, dropped a whopping 89 percent. Although it would take the economy over a decade to recover, it took even longer for Wall Street. It wasn't until 1954 that the market had fully regained its pre-crash value.

Then there was the 1973 oil crisis and recession, with its accompanying 48 percent stock market crash. Yet it only took us about two years for the market to recover from that one.

In 1987 the Dow Jones experienced its greatest one-day loss (nearly 23 percent) on October 19, what is now referred to as "Black Monday." This is also sometimes called a *mini-crash*, because—while it took nearly two years for the market to surpass pre-crash levels—it regained nearly 60 percent of the losses in only two days.

The markets were quite robust during the remainder of the twentieth century. The NASDAQ index in particular, which trades in many of the high-tech and internet stocks, had risen more than 500 percent between 1995 and 2000. While physics tells us that—thanks to gravity—what goes up must come down, there are no such hard-and-fast rules in the stock market. What goes up *may* come down. Or it may not. When the dot-com bubble burst in 2000, the stock market most certainly did come down. By 2002 NASDAQ had dropped by 77 percent, bringing down the Dow Jones and Standard & Poor's (S&P) 500 with it (though by much smaller, yet not insignificant, margins). It took NASDAQ nearly fifteen years to regain its pre-crash value.

Part of the reason for the long recovery was another crash. In 2008 the subprime mortgage crisis brought the S&P 500 down 57 percent and took the rest of the worldwide markets along for the slide. It took just under eighteen months for the markets to recover from that one, and when they did, they recovered in a big way: The years

2009 to 2020 saw one of the longest and most profitable bull markets (when consumer confidence is high and stock values rise, as opposed to bear markets, which are the opposite) in US history.

We all know what happened in 2020. When COVID-19 hit and the world shut down, stock prices dropped 34 percent. The good news is that they rebounded in a couple of months; the not-so-good news is that, with global inflation and the rising interest rates used to combat it, most economists and investors still consider the markets to be more bearish than bullish.

What goes up may come down, but—when it comes to Wall Street—what comes down must eventually go back up. That's not a hard-and-set law (like gravity), but at this point in the history of the stock market, it's a darned good bet. Stock market crashes are going to happen, and there's no predicting them. Markets rise and fall for a host of known and unknown reasons, both financial and otherwise. Yet in the two hundred years since the New York Stock Exchange was created, stock prices have always rebounded to pre-crash levels. Then they've gone up more. Over the last century, factoring in all the crashes and fluctuations and all the bear and bull markets, the annual rate of return is still positive.

At least, so far.

SURVIVING A CRASH

Most investment advisors and financial analysts and pundits are a bit like car dealers: They'll tout amazing and cutting-edge "safety features" and go on endlessly about how their vehicles are your best bet for surviving an accident. They'll never tell you the obvious—that the number one way to avoid a crash is to stay off the road.

I'm not saying you shouldn't drive—or invest in the markets. I'm saying that the more of your wealth you have tied up in the market (the more time you spend behind the wheel), the less safe you are. That's why having a diversified portfolio is crucial not only to *growing* your wealth but to *protecting* it.

We'll dive much further into various investment vehicles—including stocks—in the next section.

THE GOOD, THE BAD, AND THE DEADLY: MARKET FLUCTUATIONS AND THE SEQUENCE OF RETURNS RISK

For those who are wisely invested and still in their prime earning years, market fluctuations—up or down—are a part of doing business. When stock values are up, you're making money; when values are down, you're provided with opportunities to buy shares cheaper. Most wise investors don't fret over the daily ticker, secure in the knowledge that—historically and statistically—the odds for growth are in your favor. Time is on your side.

It's kind of like with your home. Some time ago I found this 24-hour "Real Estate Values" network on TV. On this channel, they ran a ticker, 24/7, showing changes in real estate values minute by minute, in real time.

My question, spoken out loud to the TV, was "Why?"

Unless you're selling your home (or looking to buy), what possible good can come from paying any attention to that? I've lived in my home for many years. I'm not planning to sell it anytime soon. I'm pretty sure it's worth substantially more than it was when I bought it. I know that, if I do decide to sell it at some point, it will probably be worth even more then. I also know that there will be times—as its value rises—when the value of my home drops. That's the nature of the real estate market. I don't sweat it. As an investor in my home, I'm in it for the long haul.

Just as my interest in the day-to-day fluctuations of the real estate market would drastically change if I were to put my house up for sale and use the proceeds to fund my living costs, so, too, does everything change when your investments become not a vehicle for growth but a vehicle for survival.

When you retire, time is no longer on your side.

This is when the stock market is the most perilous, thanks in no small part to a little financial principle known as the *sequence of returns* risk.

When the dot-com bubble burst in 2000, it wiped out the retirement accounts of untold thousands of seniors across America. Their dreams of enjoying their golden years traveling and spending time with grandkids evaporated.

They had to keep working. More than a few of them are still working.

Why? Sequence of returns.

Contrary to popular belief, if the market goes down 10 or 15 percent, you don't gain it back with a subsequent 10 or 15 percent rebound. Let's say your stock portfolio has $100,000 in it, and the market drops 10 percent. Now you have $90,000. A 10 percent rebound then only brings you back to $99,000. The market is up as much as it went down, but you've still lost $1,000. To get back to even, the market must increase more than it decreased. Now let's say that you're no longer growing your wealth but relying on your investment portfolio to live. That's another hit, requiring an even greater market rebound to get back to where you started.

And, to paraphrase Tom Cruise from *A Few Good Men*, the hits will keep on coming—unless the markets get real bullish real quick. After you've sold too many shares and the account can never recover, you either run out of money and move in with the kids or go back to work just to survive.

MORE ON SURVIVING A CRASH

In addition to, as I mentioned earlier, having a diverse investment portfolio that doesn't rely too heavily on the fluctuations of the stock market, there are three things that can greatly reduce the odds of a crash being fatal. If you have at least one of these, your odds of walking away intact will be improved dramatically. If you have all three, you'll be even safer—and more likely to come out ahead on the other side.

A GUARANTEED INCOME

A guaranteed income might be a pension, an annuity (covered earlier), Social Security, or, most likely, some combination thereof. The key is to have a "floor" of income not tied to market fluctuations that you can't outlive. Ideally, this would be enough to cover your required living expenses.

PERMANENT LIFE INSURANCE

As I discussed in the last chapter, permanent life insurance policies build up a cash value that can be borrowed against or withdrawn from, if you so desire. When equity values drop, these values can be accessed to cover living expenses while you wait for the inevitable market recovery.

A HOME

Your home can be your shelter from the storm—not only literally but financially. All those years of mortgage payments have been an investment and have created equity, thanks to those payments and the increase in value of the home. That equity can be used—through a home equity loan or a reverse mortgage—to get you through the types of storms that don't damage the roof.

Having at least one—and preferably all three—of these protections in place can give you the freedom to pursue a more aggressive investment strategy for those assets above and beyond your cost of living to turn "What if the market crashes?" to "So what when the market crashes?"

5

WHAT IF INTEREST RATES SOAR?

Interest rates have been in the news a lot lately.

Why? Because they're going up.

The Federal Reserve, the US government's central bank, raises and lowers interest rates as a way to try to keep America's economy at least reasonably stable. When economic growth is sluggish, rates are lowered to stimulate spending. When the economy grows too much—and the government spends too much—the result is often inflation. The Fed then raises interest rates in an attempt to dissuade people from spending. Inflation is nothing more than too many dollars chasing too few goods. Higher interest rates can help decrease demand and cut consumer spending.

In case you hadn't noticed, inflation is pretty high (at the time of this writing, it's about 8 percent). You would have to go back over forty years to see a higher inflation rate (in 1980, it hit nearly 15 percent). So, in response, interest rates have been rocketing back up again.

The good news is that it's pretty unlikely that interest rates will, at least in the foreseeable future, climb to their March 1980 peak of 20 percent. The bad news is that few predicted they would hit 20 percent in the first place. What we all need is a strategy in place that can withstand the highest of highs and the lowest of lows, whether those highs and lows are related to interest rates, inflation, or the equity markets. A strategy that, in effect, accentuates the positive and mitigates the negative.

HOW RISING INTEREST RATES AFFECT YOUR WEALTH

STOCKS AND BONDS

Typically, higher interest rates have an inverse relationship to the stock market: Higher interest rates lead to a decline in the prices of stocks. Higher interest rates significantly (and negatively) impact long-term bonds. We'll talk more about these in the next section of the book.

PROPERTY VALUES

Interest rates drive the value of properties as well, whether you're selling or buying. A few points of interest either way can mean a difference of tens of thousands of dollars in the cost of purchasing property, which (obviously) affects the demand.

MORTGAGES

There are two types of home mortgages: fixed and variable. Fixed loans have a set term (usually fifteen, twenty, or thirty years), and the loan amortization (payment installments over time) and interest rates are set at the time the loan is created. In a period of increasing interest rates and inflation, the fixed mortgage is priceless. The bank cannot change the rate, and the effective cost of the loan is reduced relative to inflation.

On the other hand, variable- and adjustable-rate loans also have a fixed term for the amortization but an adjustable term for the interest rates. When interest rates rise, so does your monthly payment. These loans have a cap on both the period and the life of the loan interest rate increases. These can be dangerous if you bought your property based on a low rate, and rates rise while you hold the loan.

These types of loans usually have a lower rate at the time they're issued than fixed-rate loans, making them beneficial if you don't think you'll be living in the home for the rest of your life. For instance, when I bought my first home, I thought I might live there for five or six years, so I got a five-year adjustable loan, which locked in my interest rate for five years. After that, it would adjust up or down depending on the market. As I didn't think I was going to be there that long, it made more sense than paying the higher (at the time) thirty-year fixed rate.

SAVINGS ACCOUNTS AND CERTIFICATES OF DEPOSIT (CD)

While rising interest rates generally have a negative impact on the value of stocks, bonds, and property, they can be a good thing for your savings accounts and CDs because they can be benefactors of the increasing cost of money. Not all banks, however, will follow the Fed's lead when interest rates rise, which can come as an unpleasant surprise to the bank's savings account and CD holders. If your savings are in one of those banks, this might be an awesome time to shop around.

WHOLE LIFE INSURANCE

When interest rates rise, the cash value of your whole life insurance policy can increase faster as well. The insurance company has the opportunity to invest in long-term bonds that pay a higher interest rate, so they're getting a higher return. If you own the policies with a mutual insurance company (one in which policyholders share in company profits), you will too.

CREDIT CARDS, PERSONAL LOANS, AND AUTO LOANS

If you're a borrower at times of increasing interest rates, your cost to use credit can increase almost instantly as the Fed shifts policy. As a result, the rate on your credit cards would go up monthly, making paying off the balances in full more critical than ever.

Home equity lines of credit would see similar rapid increases and, unless you have a fixed-rate loan, your payments will be continuously increasing.

While car loan payments, once secured, will not increase, buying the car will get more expensive every time you go to the dealer. This is true whether you finance the purchase or not.

Each of these increases in cost could cut into your cash flow budget or annual savings and investment allotments. If this happens in retirement, and the market is down at the time, see chapter 4 for what this could mean for your future spending hopes and desires.

As you can see, rising interest rates can create challenges in all aspects of wealth management. But challenges can also create opportunities. The right advisor—who's able to see the big picture—can be the difference between sour lemons and delicious, refreshing lemonade.

6

WHAT IF THE GOVERNMENT TRIES TO TAKE MORE OF MY STUFF?

In November 1789, in a letter to French scientist Jean-Baptiste Le Roy, Benjamin Franklin wrote what many historians consider to be his "last great quote": "Our new Constitution is now established, everything seems to promise it will be durable; but, in this world, nothing is certain except death and taxes."[2]

Less than five months later, Franklin, proving the accuracy of at least part of that statement, succumbed to pleurisy at the age of eighty-four.

Taxation, like the United States itself, has greatly evolved since Benjamin Franklin's time. When we gained our independence from England, tax collection was limited to tariffs, a tax on whiskey and (briefly) glass windows, and various

---

2   NCC Staff, "Benjamin Franklin's last great quote and the Constitution," constitutioncenter.org, November 13, 2021. https://constitutioncenter.org/blog/benjamin-franklins-last-great-quote-and-the-constitution

poll, property, and excise taxes. Things like inheritance and sales taxes weren't added until the twentieth century, much like (with the exception of a brief period during the Civil War) federal income tax.

A recent study published on the website Self.inc estimated—using an assortment of available national and state data—that the average American will spend one-third of their lifetime earnings paying taxes.[3]

We pay so much in taxes because governments—local, state, and federal—keep spending more money on more stuff, and only so much money can be printed before inflation starts getting out of control (as we've recently seen). So we pay taxes on almost everything. We pay taxes on the money we earn, then we pay taxes again when we spend it. We pay taxes on utilities, property, capital gains, stock dividends, earned interest, gasoline, cell phones, airline travel, and hotels. We pay taxes for living, then we pay taxes again when we die. With the exception of a few assets and life insurance payouts, our heirs pay income taxes on the money we leave behind. Even with life insurance, our heirs are still paying taxes on everything they buy with the proceeds. Also, depending on the value of one's estate, estate taxes could be levied on it all.

Benjamin Franklin had a point. He just didn't know how *much* of a point.

---

3   "A Life of Tax: What will Americans pay in tax over their lifetime?" self.inc, accessed November 20, 2023, https://www.self.inc/info/life-of-tax/.

And guess what? It's not going to get any better. There isn't an economist worth their salt predicting a future with fewer taxes. It could happen, but I wouldn't bet on it.

The question shouldn't be "What if the government tries to take more of my stuff?" Rather, it should be, "What do I do when the government tries to take more of my stuff?" Because I assure you, they will.

The right plan going forward relies on tax strategies to ensure that you're not paying a dime more in taxes than necessary. And these strategies are implemented at every phase of your financial life: They protect your wealth from burdensome taxation, they grow your wealth with less burdensome taxation, they allow you to enjoy your wealth (spending your money on things other than taxes is way more fun), and they transfer your wealth in a way that protects your heirs from the aforementioned burdensome taxation.

This isn't dodging your taxes or not paying your fair share. As we've established, if you earn and spend money in the United States, you're going to pay your fair share. And then some. Nor is there anything shady about it. Taxes are, by design, complex. The IRS tax code contains thousands upon thousands of pages. Buried in those pages are many ways to pay less, but the IRS certainly isn't going to help you find them. The same can be said for your state and local governments. Navigating the labyrinth of legalese—and keeping track of the perpetual changes and how they affect your bottom line—is the job of your financial advisory team.

As we go through the rest of this book, I'll tell you more about some of these different strategies and how they can be leveraged to make Uncle Sam unhappy—but keep you happier.

SECTION II

GROW YOUR WEALTH

UNDERSTANDING (AND MAKING THE MOST OF) INVESTMENTS

In the introduction I mentioned that successful wealth management requires looking at the "big picture" and how each component of your unique situation and your goals plays a role in your family's and your long-term happiness. I told you that, unfortunately, most financial advisors aren't trained and knowledgeable enough in all the elements of your big picture to do that.

They usually keep that to themselves.

These folks often only wear one hat, and they only have a single tool in their toolbox. And as I also said in the introduction, if all you have is a hammer, everything is going to look like a nail. For a large number of these advisors, it's all about growth. It's all about investments.

That's the hat they wear. That's the hammer in their toolbox.

In this section we're going to talk about your investments and the role they play in successful wealth management. We'll discuss different types of investments and how they fit into the big picture.

Chances are you'll learn some things your investment advisor won't tell you about—things that aren't on their hat rack or in their toolbox because they're ignorant of the opportunity.

7

INVESTING 101

Just for fun, I googled "books on investing." Take a guess how many results I got.

Hundreds of thousands?

Maybe a few million?

Nope. As I'm writing this, on an early morning in January 2023, there were over two billion results for this particular query. (Google found these in 0.7 seconds because, you know, the internet.)

That doesn't mean there are really over two billion books about investing. After all, my search parameter was rather broad. But you get the point: A lot of books have been written on the subject. Good luck reading them before your will matures.

This book isn't a "book on investing." (Although if you do the same search, you'll likely find me in there somewhere.)

Your financial future is about more than investing; rather, it's about using investments as part of a broader strategy to effectively protect, grow, enjoy, and, eventually, transfer your wealth in a way that brings you the most happiness and well-being.

When it comes down to it, there are two key components to investing: understanding the different options (what you're investing in) and determining where to invest so that it best serves the broader strategy.

UNDERSTANDING YOUR OPTIONS

What do we even mean by "investing"? At its heart, the word means the same thing regardless of the context in which it's used. Simply put, investing is an expenditure made in the hopes of reaping a greater reward. In the case of earning a degree or learning a skill, it's usually an expenditure of both money and time. Same with starting a business (hence the term "sweat equity").

As we get older and our investments in education, mastering a trade, or building a business begin reaping rewards, the "time" part of the equation becomes more and more precious. We begin seeking ways to grow our wealth that are more focused on the "money" part (earned through time already invested). We start thinking more about investment vehicles such as stocks and bonds (what most people think of when they hear the word "invest," and where 99 percent of investment advisors will try to steer you [the hat and the toolbox]), money market accounts, CDs and savings accounts, and real estate. We might also think of less-traditional vehicles such as art, precious metals, promising new start-ups, or even riskier (at the time of this writing) vehicles like cryptocurrencies.

Most of these are passive investments: You put your money in and watch it grow. Or not. There's nothing wrong with that. Although some will call it "lazy investing," the truth is, as mentioned, you probably invested plenty of time earning the money that you're investing.

In later chapters, I'll break down for you exactly what these passive investments are all about and how they can play a role in your successful wealth management. But we'll also talk about active investing. These investments will require more time, but it can be quality time that enriches both your happiness and bank account. Active investing can be, in short, more fun. And profitable.

WHERE TO INVEST

There are always investment opportunities. A lot of them. Google turned up 1.3 billion. Even if you eliminate all the scam artists (something I would love to do), you're still going to have a slew of opportunities for real growth. Where you invest is going to be a decision based specifically on your situation, your goals, your age, your wealth, and a host of factors that, taken together, are as unique to you as your fingerprints.

Those 99 percent of advisors I told you about aren't going to take most of these factors into account.

I do every day.

8

Cash, CDs, and Bank Accounts

When it comes to protecting wealth, many Americans do it the old-fashioned way. They open a savings account, they put funds into CDs or money market accounts, or they stuff some cash under the mattress or in a cookie jar. They reason that—while it may not grow significantly in a bank (and even less under the mattress)—at least their money will be safe. It won't lose value.

They look at the risks inherent in stocks, bonds, real estate, and other investments and weigh it against the risk that the banking system and Federal Deposit Insurance Corporation will collapse, or that they'll lose their house (and mattress or cookie jar) in a fire, flood, or storm. They figure that their way is a better bet.

What they don't realize is that liquid assets—whether in a bank or squirreled away at home—do lose value. That money erodes as surely as if you had put it in a paper bag and buried it in your garden.

How? The answer is hidden in plain sight. It's not really hidden at all—we hear about it all the time. It rears its ugly head every time we go to the store or make a purchase online.

I'll bet you know where I'm going with this.

Yep. Inflation.

The constantly increasing cost of living, that insidious tax that offers neither breaks nor loopholes, means that—with every passing day or week or month—the value of the money in those "safe" repositories diminishes.

The last year has been particularly damaging in that regard, but inflation always has been and always will be. It will rise and it will fall, but it will never go away—a stealth tax that hits the poor and middle class the hardest.

"But what about interest?" you ask. "Won't the rising rates also lift the value of my savings?"

Yes, it will. Just not enough.

First, the interest earned from your savings accounts, money market accounts, or CDs would have to be greater than the rate of inflation in order to stop the bleeding. As of this writing, the average yield for a traditional savings account is less than 1 percent. Significantly less. CDs are a little better—the average interest for one of those is currently between 4 and 5 percent.

Last I checked, mattresses and cookie jars pay no interest at all.

Second, there's rarely a direct correlation between the Fed's interest rate and the interest paid by financial institutions. There's almost always going to be a lag time and—even if your bank does raise its rates for savings accounts—it most assuredly won't match the Fed's rate. Banks are, above all else, in business to make money.

CDs have their interest rates set at the time of purchase.

Does this mean that I always steer my clients away from savings accounts, CDs, mattresses, and cookie jars?

Not at all. Wealth management requires looking at the big picture. Having such liquid assets (like cash or savings) can play an important role in your overall financial strategy. They can act as a safety net or can even be used as a tool for future growth. It all depends on your unique situation and goals.

Just don't think of them as an investment. They're not.

9

BONDS

As I mentioned earlier, when many Americans think of tools for growing wealth, they think of stocks and bonds. Those two investment vehicles are often mentioned in the same breath: *stocks and bonds*. Like *peanut butter and jelly* or *bacon and eggs*—as if the two things naturally go together (now I'm getting hungry).

Like peanut butter and jelly or bacon and eggs, stocks and bonds can go together. As part of a diversified investment portfolio, they can be a yummy part of your wealth management diet. But they're different beasts.

We'll discuss stocks in the next chapter. For now, let's talk bonds.

WHAT IS A BOND?

When you buy a bond, you're essentially making a loan. You're acting, in this sense, like a bank or other lending institution—providing money in exchange for a promise from the borrower to pay it all back *with interest*. In the case of bonds, the borrower—whether an individual, a corporation, the government, or foreign governments—holds on to the principal (the amount borrowed) for the term of the bond (anywhere from three months to thirty years) and pays you the interest in regular disbursements throughout that term. At the conclusion of that period of time—when the bond matures—the borrower promises to pay back the loan in full.

For example, if you buy a $100,000 bond at 3 percent interest for a term of ten years, you're going to get paid $3,000 per year for that ten-year term. After that, you'll get back the full $100,000.

Pretty neat, huh?

Well, unless the borrowing entity (again, the bond seller) goes under or defaults. Then all you get is the interest they've paid to that point.

Not too neat, huh?

Then there are taxes. I know, I know . . . hard to believe.

DIFFERENT BONDS, DIFFERENT RATES, AND DIFFERENT TAXES

If you buy a bond from a business entity (like a corporation), you're going to owe federal and, where applicable, state income taxes on the interest payments you receive, as if you had earned that money from a job. These types of bonds are usually going to offer the highest interest rates because they're typically the riskiest (the greatest chance of default).

For US Treasury bonds (or bonds issued by other US governmental agencies), you have to pay federal—but not state—income tax on the interest earned. Bonds issued by states or municipalities where you don't live won't be charged federal income tax on the interest, but you'll still have to pay the income tax of your state (if applicable). Bonds issued by foreign governments are pretty much like a bond issued by a business or corporation—federal and state income tax will apply to the interest they pay.

About the only types of bonds excluded from any type of income tax on the interest earned are municipal bonds issued by the state or municipality you live in. But guess what? These types of bonds also typically pay the lowest rates.

As you might imagine with something as complex as the US tax code, there are exceptions to everything I told you about the taxation of earnings from interest. For example, if those bonds are in retirement accounts, it can earn interest inside that account—to potentially be used for other investments—and is not taxed until such a time as you withdraw it. Sometimes, not even then.

As with almost every element of your winning financial strategy, you shouldn't try this at home.

MORE ON THOSE INTEREST RATES

We briefly talked in chapter 5 about the relationship of interest rates to the value of bonds and how rising interest rates can significantly and negatively affect their value. Much of it depends on timing.

Because the interest rates on bonds are locked in for the duration of the term, if rates rise during that term, the bonds are worth less—not only because you'll get less should you need to sell these bonds before maturity, but also because you'll be earning less than you would have if you bought the same bonds while the rates were up. Conversely, if you invest in bonds during times of relatively high interest rates, they'll be worth more if rates drop, for exactly the same reasons.

Way back when, in 1981, the US government was offering thirty-year T-bonds ("Treasury" bonds) that paid just over 15 percent interest. Putting $100,000 into these bonds would have paid more than $15,000 per year over the next three decades (that's over $450,000 total), with the principal returned to you at the end of the term, which would have been in 2011. That's a return of over 450 percent! Yet not a whole lot of folks purchased these bonds. The economy was a wreck. The forecasters were predicting rates would climb even higher and that you would have been better to wait until that arrived.

They were wrong.

Now we know (because hindsight is twenty-twenty) that they had reached their ceiling. So far, at least. Those same bonds in 2020 would have yielded 1.5 percent interest, or $1,500 annually. About enough to pay for your daily

Starbucks (if you don't get too fancy). As I write this, the Feds just raised the interest rate by another quarter-percentage point. Thirty-year T-bonds are offering just over 3.5 percent interest. Still a far cry from 1981, but more than double from a year ago.

The interest rates available on bonds vary greatly. The example above is for thirty-year US Treasury bonds. Those rates are usually less with each successive shortening of the term (i.e., a twenty-year bond will pay less than a thirty-year, a ten-year even less than that). Because these bonds are backed by the full faith and credit of the US government (and despite the nagging, persistent flirtation with government default), they're still considered the safest bonds you can buy.

As with most investments, there is a direct correlation between risk and reward. That's how the market works: If we loan money to (buy bonds from) Ma and Pa Jones for their new business venture, we're going to want a better return than if we buy bonds from Apple. The greater the chance of default, the greater the reward. Ma and Pa Jones could become the next Apple—after all, this is America—and the returns on our investment could be phenomenal. But the odds are against it. And the risk that they'll close up shop while holding our bond is that much greater. That's why such high-risk/high-yield bonds are often called *junk bonds*. No offense to Ma and Pa Jones.

IT'S ALL ABOUT DIVERSIFICATION

I've said it before, I'll say it now (and I'll say it later as well): The best financial strategy is about so much more than any single investment, or even type of investment (contrary to what many of the financial gurus will tell you). It's about a long-term strategy to protect, grow, enjoy, and—ultimately— transfer your wealth by looking at the big picture of your unique situation, goals, and dreams. There is no one-size-fits-all, and there is definitely no silver bullet. Your wealth management team's toolbox has to have more than a hammer.

Diversification, in all elements of this strategy, is the right prescription. Your portfolio could include a combination of high-yield (more risky) and low-yield (less risky) bonds of different-length terms. (As a general rule, you should buy short-term bonds if you believe interest rates are going up and for risk mitigation, and only buy long-term bonds if you believe rates are going down.)

Of course, you don't have to invest in individual bonds (or, honestly, *any* bonds). There are investment companies out there that pool clients' money into a mutual fund that only invests in certain types of bonds, whether it's short-term, relatively safe government bonds; long-term, riskier junk bonds; or anything in between.

Bonds can be safe. They can be risky. They can grow your wealth substantially, or they can barely grow it at all. You can make money; you can lose money. Everything in life has, to a certain degree, an element of risk. Proper investing isn't about avoiding risk—it's about avoiding unnecessary risk.

Calculated risk is worth the opportunity.

Which is a wonderful way to introduce you to stocks.

10

STOCKS

When it comes to investing for most Americans, the stock market is "the show." Love it or hate it (and I do both, depending on the situation), it's what most folks in this country invest in.

I don't mean most investors. I mean most people. Surveys have shown that, in 2022, more than half of all adult Americans—58 percent—had at least some involvement in the stock market. The all-time high for the percentage of the population owning stocks was in 2007, when that number reached a whopping 67 percent. I'll bet you can guess why that number dropped precipitously shortly thereafter (it rhymes with "crash").

Many of these investors have money in some sort of retirement account that invests in the market in order to grow those funds. Some invest as a hobby—they have a few bucks to play with after they've paid their bills and see the stock market as a safer alternative to buying lottery tickets or going to the casino (it definitely is that).

Stocks can play a role, directly or indirectly, in almost every facet of a winning wealth management strategy. Or it can play little to no role. Chances are you won't hear that from most investment advisors, who will shout from the mountaintops (or on YouTube) that the stock market is the Holy Grail.

To use market vernacular, they're selling you short.

THE DIFFERENCE BETWEEN STOCKS AND BONDS

As I told you in the last chapter, buying bonds is loaning a company (or government) money. You have no say in what that entity does with the money—you fork over the dough and collect the interest payments. With stocks, on the other hand, you're buying a piece of the company. (Governments don't sell stocks. If they did, you might have more than a few countries—including our own—in the hands of private investors. Whether that's what's actually happening is a political debate we won't get into here.)

Owning stock in a company means that you're one of the owners of that company, entitled to a share of the after-tax profits commensurate with the number of shares you own. You can also have a voice in the way the company handles that money, again to the extent of the proportion of your holdings. You're likely not going to own enough shares to get the ear of the board of directors, but you do have more of a voice than if you had bought a bond and loaned the company money.

TWO TYPES OF STOCK VALUES

The value of each of your shares of stock is divided into two different categories: *book value* and *market value*. The former is what the actual physical company—all its assets, such as buildings, equipment, office furniture, computers, et cetera—would be worth if the company were to sell everything today. If a company has $1 billion in total assets and has 1 billion shares of stock outstanding, each share has a book value of a buck.

That's not the value that gets folks excited. That's not the reason most people invest in the stock market. That would be the market value.

The market value of my share of stock is based on what people believe the stock is going to be worth in the future. If enough folks believe that same company is going to be worth $10 billion down the road (based on earnings, future profitability, and a host of other unknown factors), those same billion shares we talked about are going to be worth ten bucks each. Voila! You've increased the value of your share by 1,000 percent.

Congratulations!

But nobody has a crystal ball. At least not one that's anywhere close to accurate. Remember: There was once a time when Betamax was doing quite well. On any given day there are people who are right and people who are wrong. Nobody ever knows for sure, because the whole ball of wax is based on a future that isn't here yet. One person might believe the company's future isn't quite so rosy; they may think the company is going to decrease in value. If they own shares in the company, they might want to sell. Obviously, they'll want to sell to someone who thinks the company's future is brighter than they think it is.

That, in a nutshell, is the stock market. If you've ever seen the floor of the New York Stock Exchange during trading, you'll know that *nutshell* is an appropriate way to describe it. At least the *nuts* part.

DIVIDENDS

You don't necessarily need to sell your stock for more than you paid for it in order to profit from those shares. Many companies will, from time to time, offer what are known as *dividends* to their stockholders. Going back to our previous example: That billion-dollar company that most believe will, in the future, be worth $10 billion can choose to pay stock-holders a 5 percent dividend. In our case that share that's now worth ten dollars is going to earn a fifty-cent dividend for each share. You can keep the cash and do with it whatever you please, or you could use that money to re-invest. If you hold the stock inside of a retirement account, like an individual retirement account (IRA), 401(k), 403(b), or Roth IRA, these dividends will grow tax deferred and may be taxed as ordinary income later, upon withdrawal. If you own the stock, the dividends will be taxed when received.

SMALLER CAN BE BETTER

The sizes of companies offering stock shares run the gamut. Those with assets under $1 billion are considered "small cap," those worth $1–10 billion are "mid-cap," and those above $10 billion are considered "large cap." Most investment advisors, however, will steer you toward the "giants," the big names such as Amazon, Starbucks, Google, and Apple. Even if you invest on your own, you may well be drawn to the most visible and well-known names. This is known as *familiarity bias*. That and a host of other biases cause people to invest in these stocks.

But did you know that, historically, smaller stocks outperform the giants? Yes, there's more risk, but that's why there's a greater possible reward. Think about it: If you had bought $10,000 in Amazon stock in 1997 (when the company was getting started), you could have sold it in 2017 for $6.7 million. If, on the other hand, you bought Amazon stock in 2020 . . . I don't have to tell you that as of this writing you've lost money.

You're probably not going to find the next Amazon, but a competent wealth management team will hopefully be knowledgeable enough about the academic facts of investing to at least give you your best shot over time to create better results.

AGAIN WITH THE DIVERSIFICATION

As with any investment, your best chances lie not in picking exactly the right stocks to buy, but in buying a wide enough range that those earning money will more than offset the losses of those that don't. That's what a "diversified stock portfolio" is. Additionally, trying to pick individual stocks is always speculating and gambling with your money, and it's almost never a winning strategy.

A better way for you to accomplish this is through a mutual fund (which I briefly covered in the last chapter) or exchange-traded fund (ETF). Mutual funds and ETFs are operated by professional money managers (including many financial firms that are household names) who allocate the fund's assets across a wide range of the stocks in the fund's portfolio, and your rewards (and risks) are shared among the rest of the investors in that fund. Rather than putting all your eggs in one basket, you're investing in someone else's basket—you play no role in choosing the eggs.

But this doesn't have to be the extent of your diversification. You can have a diversified investment portfolio that includes—but isn't limited to—the diversified portfolio of a mutual fund. These funds can hold large and small stocks,

US and foreign stocks, and value and growth stocks in a few different baskets. It's like putting your eggs in a basket that also holds a different basket. Or a few different baskets. (At the time of this writing, any basket filled with actual eggs is going to be fairly valuable in its own right.)

A CAUTIONARY TALE

Back in the late nineties, when I had been in the business for about ten years, the tech bubble was still growing strong. Investors were going crazy sinking funds into what I call "bags of air"— buying tech stocks in companies that didn't have any current earnings, profits, or prospects for either of those in the near future. I had a client, a good guy with a great job, whom we had helped with life insurance and some good, solid, non-tech diversified investments, the latter of which was growing at a steady rate of 8–10 percent.

Our client received a tip about a guy—one who worked for a well-known investment firm—who could grow his money faster with tech stocks. He started with a portfolio of about $5 million and took about $1 million out of our account and invested with the new guy.

That investment grew by 45 percent in one year. Our client, with dollar signs in his eyes, invested another $3 million. This time the return was 70 percent for the next year. He then took the remaining funds out of the account invested with us and invested with the other guy. I implored him not to put all his eggs in that basket, but he—like so many other investors at the time—was in love with that basket.

Sadly, we all know what happened to that basket. Within a year of the tech bubble bursting in the early 2000s, his total investment account was down over 90 percent and was worth less than half a million dollars. Not only did he lose almost his entire nest egg, he also lost out on all the opportunities provided by the bull market (one of the longest in history) that followed. The retirement and the future he had hoped for—for him and his family—never occurred. There's never a good time to speculate and gamble with your money.

Don't be like that client. Diversify, mitigate stock market risk with short-term bonds, rebalance your portfolio (which we'll talk about more in the next chapter), and remember the lesson of "The Tortoise and the Hare." Slow and steady wins this race.

11

ALLOCATION
AND REBALANCING

As I've mentioned (quite a few times already), diversification—not putting all your investment eggs in one basket—is a crucial component of any winning wealth management strategy. It would be nice to tell you "It's as simple as that," but it's not. Yes, a diversified portfolio is important, but what *really* matters is how it is diversified—how much you have invested in what.

We're going to talk about that in this chapter.

ALLOCATION

If you've ever made out a monthly budget—and I'm sure you have—you're allocating your income. Part of the check will go to rent or mortgage, part to utilities, part to monthly premium payments on your various types of insurance, part to car maintenance and fuel, part to groceries and entertainment, and part to other bills. Some of these allocations—like your rent or mortgage and insurance premiums—are etched in stone. They're not going to fluctuate wildly and unexpectedly. Others—like many of your utilities, your car's fuel bill, and your groceries—can fluctuate (sometimes, as we've seen with groceries and gas, wildly and unexpectedly).

As you might guess, the markets are more like groceries and gas.

Investment assets are generally divided into different "classes"—like equities (e.g., stocks), fixed income (e.g., bonds), cash and cash equivalents, real estate, commodities, et cetera. Then there are "subclasses" of each asset class. Stocks can be large or small, value or growth, and domestic or foreign. Bonds can have short-term, mid-term, and long-term maturities and can range from super high quality (e.g., government bonds) to super high risk (aka junk/high-yield bonds). These subclasses often behave similarly to one another in the marketplace; however, the distinct asset classes behave dissimilarly. This is known as *correlation*.

Correlation is not the friend of a truly diversified portfolio. You may think that, because you have your assets spread across a wide range of stocks, you're diversified. Not really.

A better strategy—and what makes for a truly diversified portfolio—is to have your investments spread out among different classes and subclasses so that losses from one class are more than offset by gains in another. Not because you *believe* that one class is going to outperform another. That's crystal ball investing, and, as I said earlier, you don't have a crystal ball. Neither does your investment advisor. If he or she tries to make you believe otherwise, run!

Your wealth management team should help you develop a *target asset allocation*, one which uses a long-term, academic, evidence-based approach to investing. Your allocation should take into account factors such as your age, your timeline, your risk tolerance and capacity, and the level of return commensurate with the risk you're willing to accept.

Once your allocation is established, you can't set it and forget it. You have to have the discipline to rebalance your portfolio over time.

REBALANCING

Maintaining your target asset allocation requires periodically buying or selling assets to keep your portfolio in alignment for long-term risk management.

Convincing a client to take money (some, not all) from an investment that's currently up and put it into something that's not doing as well (or even going down) is one of the hardest things I do. There's a certain addictive thrill in the "ups." If anything, they'll usually want to invest more.

Wise investors—and the best wealth managers—know better. They're looking at the big picture, at the 30,000-foot view. As you'll recall from the last chapter, I begged my tech-bubble client to rebalance his portfolio more prudently, to resist the temptation to put all his eggs in that tech basket. He ignored me. You know how that turned out.

Stocks go up. Stocks go down. So do bonds. So does every type of investment. Otherwise, they wouldn't be "investments." Long-term growth doesn't come from knee-jerk reactions to current market fluctuations but from informed, evidence-based, big-picture strategies that will not only help you grow but protect and *enjoy* your wealth.

Less anxiety. Less stress. Less risk. More enjoyment.

12

Participatory Investing

So far in this section on growth, we've covered the more traditional investments. As I alluded to earlier, these types of financial vehicles can be thought of as glorified holding accounts: You may be actively involved in deciding where and when your money is invested, but you generally have no control over how it's used by those entities in which it's invested.

There's nothing wrong with that. These investments are traditional for a reason—this is the path most investors choose.

But it's not the only path. Far from it.

There's a whole world of investment opportunities out there that offer not only an opportunity for growth but also a chance to experience the fulfillment of getting your hands dirty by being involved in that growth.

This is called *participatory investing*, and most investment advisors won't say a peep about it. They don't get paid to help you put your money into these vehicles. It's like I said earlier: If you only have a hammer in your toolbox, everything is going to be a nail.

If you're a business owner, you know all about participatory investing—it's what you've been doing for as long as you've owned your business. If you're a homeowner, you've been doing this with every renovation you've made to your house through the years. Although to varying degrees, both of these are participatory investments. You put in the money, you do the work, and the value of your investment hopefully grows.

Participatory investing allows you to put your money where your heart is. And chances are, if you truly love doing something, you're probably pretty darned good at it.

Love home renovation? Buy distressed real estate, fix it up, then sell it (known as *flipping*) or turn it into rental property.

Love art? If you're an art aficionado, there's money to be made in art investing that doesn't necessarily require that you purchase a Picasso.

Love exotic cars? There are owners of such vehicles who have created Airbnb-type companies that turn a profit renting fancy vehicles to those who might not be able to buy them but will pay a pretty penny to rent them for a day or a weekend. Oh, and by the way, if you go this route, you get to drive them when they're not being rented.

Love movies? I've helped people find investments in independent film production companies that have made them money.

The list goes on and on, limited only by your imagination.

Here's a dirty little secret you'll seldom hear from the investment experts: While, overall, the risks of such participatory investments are greater than the risks of the traditional routes, the rewards can be much greater. Almost exponentially so. And the financial rewards are only a small part of the equation. Ask any successful entrepreneur—they'll tell you the same thing.

I've invested in rental firms, hotels, vacation resorts, all sorts of commercial and residential real estate, other small start-up businesses, and even movies. I've made some money; I've lost some money. But these investments—when successful—gave me much greater satisfaction than my more traditional investments in stocks and bonds. I loved having an active role in their success (even if only in an advisory capacity). There's nothing like it. Even when one of these investments didn't pan out like I had hoped, the knowledge gained through trying and the relationships built along the way have made it worthwhile.

I've steered clients toward many participatory investments where I didn't stand to earn a dime. Yet because I prefer working with individuals and families, providing true wealth management, my success comes from their long-term success. It isn't necessary (or sometimes even prudent) to limit their opportunities for growth to my short-term profit.

Successful growth—like successful wealth management itself—is far more complex and multifaceted than putting your money into the right stocks and bonds. It's about factoring the hopes, dreams, and financial goals of not just you but your family into a long-term, big-picture strategy.

It's about living the dream. My dream—to which I've devoted an entire career—is to help you live yours. Depending on your specific situation and goals, participatory investing can hit the right spot.

Enjoy Your Wealth

The Existential Crucial Component

David Henry Thoreau is often credited with opining that "Wealth is the ability to fully experience life."

Whether or not the words were his, they sum up the very essence of what I do. I help individuals, families, and even generations of families fully experience life. And, through my work, I'm able to do the same.

How does wealth help us to fully experience life? By eliminating the stress that comes with financial uncertainty through protecting our assets. By strengthening that protection with consistent, safe growth. By being able to rest easy knowing that—when we're gone—our wealth will live on to serve our heirs and provide them the opportunity for more fully experienced lives.

But let's face it: While we all want these things, they're not all we want. We want to enjoy ourselves. We want to enjoy our wealth.

In this section we're going to discuss joy. I'll show you why it's key that you determine exactly what it is you want your wealth to do, and why the time to enjoy your wealth is now. I'll also share the stories of a few real-life clients and how I factored this existential but crucial component into their lives.

13

Define What You Want Your Money to Do

In my first meeting with every new client, I ask, "What do you want from your money?"

Then I ask, "What brings you joy?"

The questions often catch them by surprise. I'm usually far from the first financial professional they've spoken with, but I'm almost always the first to ask them that. Most financial and investment advisors operate on the theory that wealth is its own reward—that the act of growing it is, in itself, the reason.

I've found that to be far from the truth. There are those whose greatest satisfaction comes from watching their stock prices rise—and whose greatest dismay comes from watching them fall—but they're by far the exception (and not our clients).

For most of my clients, the answer to the first question is either "I want to retire and not have to worry about money."

or "I want to be able to help my children." On rare occasions it's neither of those; often it's both.

There's nothing wrong with that. Yet—while these things do bring joy (as I touched on in the opening of this section)—they are not, in and of themselves, what we really want. We really want, in the words of Thoreau, to "fully experience life."

I find it sad that so many believe they have to retire before they can do that. That so many find their careers— the more than half of our lives we spend financing our last couple of decades—as a necessary evil. Sure, there are many who like their work (at least enough to have devoted most of their lives to it). But they don't love it.

How can you tell? It's simple: Those who love their jobs don't want to retire! It's not even a concept they think about. For these folks, there is no line of demarcation between "work time" and "play time," between what they do for money and what they do to earn that money. It's exactly that passion that drives them to the heights of achievement.

Look at Warren Buffett. He reached retirement age nearly three decades ago. Same with Rupert Murdoch (although I'm guessing that perhaps the billionaire media mogul doesn't love his job quite so much in recent months).

I know, I know . . . you're neither Warren Buffett nor Rupert Murdoch. Nor am I. The point is the passion and the role it plays in a fully experienced life. I'm not going to tell you how to find passion in the job from which you've been counting down the days until retirement. But I can help you use your true passions as part of a long-term wealth management strategy that will give you purpose and enable you and your family to more fully experience life in the time you have left together.

PASSION, PURPOSE, AND LONGEVITY

It's a well-known fact (backed up by numerous studies and countless examples) that people who are fulfilled and stay productive live longer than those who don't. While we hear stories of the megasuccessful (like those mentioned above) who kept working (and, obviously, living) into their nineties, we also know of those whose golden years were short-lived, whose retirement was so unfulfilling that they lost their spark and sense of purpose.

Then they died.

We probably all know someone who lost a lifelong spouse (their passion and sense of purpose) and then followed their loved one a short time later.

These circumstances often have little to do with money. It's all about the passion and the purpose.

I want to help you find the passion and purpose that is at the heart of a fulfilled life and give you new ideas on how to leverage those passions and that purpose in ways that can also be financially fulfilling.

To echo the late, great broadcaster Paul Harvey (who worked right up until his death at age ninety), I want to help you write the *rest* of your story. It doesn't have to be a new chapter.

It can be a whole new book.

14

Don't Put Off until Tomorrow What You Can Enjoy Today

"Someday . . ."

You would be amazed at how often I hear this word from clients when talking about what they want their wealth to do for them. Investment planning or retirement planning, after all, is about the future.

They're rooted in tomorrow—in "someday."

The right wealth management, while keeping the future in mind, need not always be about someday. The key to enjoying your wealth isn't quite so far away.

In his book, "How To Stop Worrying and Start Living," Dale Carnegie wrote, "One of the most tragic things I know about human nature is that all of us tend to put off living. We are all dreaming of some magical rose garden over the horizon instead of enjoying the roses that are blooming outside our windows today."[4]

Wise man, that Mr. Carnegie. His words reflect the mindset most of my clients have about their wealth when they come to see me.

In this chapter I'm going to share with you a couple of stories about how—and why—I recommended readjusting their focus.

GOLF, FUN, AND SUN IN ARIZONA

About twenty years ago I had a successful client—a high-price, in-demand attorney around fifty years old—who had for years been sinking money into a retirement plan for that time when, fifteen years or so down the road, he was ready to slow down and enjoy some leisure time.

"My wife and I have often talked about someday owning a vacation home in Arizona," he told me.

Someday.

They had been many times (he was an avid golfer, and they both loved the climate), and they had envisioned a home there, a place to host family and friends during those months each year when many places in the country are enduring cold and snow.

"Why wait?" I asked him.

---

4   Dale Carnegie, "*How to Stop Worrying and Start Living*," New York: Simon and Schuster, 1948.

I could tell by the way he looked at me that he found the question ridiculous.

"Nobody gives us a guarantee that we're going to make it to retirement and be able to enjoy all the things we have planned for the future," I said. "With half the money you're putting into your retirement account each year, you could buy and pay the mortgage on that home now. The interest would be tax-deductible. How about you enjoy it before you retire?"

He thought for a moment. Tears welled in his eyes and then ran down his cheeks.

"You know, I never thought about it until right now," he said. "My father worked his whole life, with the dream of retiring with my mom in Florida. When the time came, they did it." He became quiet. "A year later, my father died."

I've heard similar stories countless times throughout my career. They're always heartbreaking.

Within six months he and his wife purchased a home in Arizona, on a golf course. For the remainder of his working life and beyond (he retired a few years ago), they've been enjoying long weekends with friends and vacations with their children and, now, grandchildren.

The investment in happiness also served them well financially. As you can imagine, the price they paid for the home then was significantly less than what they would have paid years down the road. If the need had arisen before he retired, he could also have used the equity in the home to get a tax-free loan, rather than paying the high taxes on an early withdrawal from the retirement account. Not only that, they rented out the home during the times they weren't using it.

Win-win-win.

PRIORITIZING PRECIOUS MEMORIES

I'm currently working with a couple—both still enjoying successful and satisfying careers—who are saving and planning for their retirement but have been dreaming of taking an Alaskan cruise with their children. All their kids are grown and in their early to mid-twenties. Two are fresh out of college and living near my clients here in Baltimore, while the youngest is currently enrolled in school in New York.

This couple worries that if they don't take this cruise soon, the chance might pass them by. They figure that once the kids are out of college and building their own careers and families, getting them together for a weeklong cruise will be like herding cats. They also worry that such an outlay of cash might adversely affect their plans for a comfortable retirement.

When they told me their dilemma, I think they were expecting me to tell them all the reasons why they shouldn't take the cruise.

If I were a typical financial advisor, they may well have been right. After all, the cost of such a trip might have lowered my earnings on the growth of that money—had it stayed put.

A typical advisor would have advised that they, too, "stay put."

So they were pleasantly surprised when I said, "Take the cruise!"

First I had to explain myself. Let's say the cruise costs $25,000. If they were to leave that money in their account and earn 6 percent net after tax for fifteen years, they would have about $60,000. Let's say, optimistically, that inflation falls and averages 4 percent per year over those fifteen years, until they're both retired and ready to take the cruise. With inflation, that cruise is now going to cost $45,000—assuming that there aren't by this time spouses and grandkids to bring along as well (an unlikely assumption). That would leave them with a maximum of about $15,000 in that account, which is certainly not going to have a major impact on their retirement. It would only generate about $600 per year, or $50 per month—not nearly enough to offset the precious years of memories they would have by taking the cruise now.

This is the kind of math my clients love.

I could tell I had made their day, and that made my day.

"Take the cruise," I repeated.

This summer, they're going to. And what did I gain financially from this specific piece of advice? Nothing.

These cases illustrate perfectly that successful wealth management isn't about protecting, growing, and—eventually—transferring your wealth. *Enjoying* your money is the thread that runs through it all.

And there's no time like the present.

15

GIVING ISN'T "GIVING BACK"

When it comes to enjoying our wealth, we often think of the happiness derived from things: homes, cars, vacations, etc. Yet one of the most endearing traits about our species is that many of us find great pleasure in giving stuff away. You may have heard the quote, often attributed to Winston Churchill, that says, "We make a living by what we get. We make a life by what we give." Most of my clients would agree.

Giving makes us happy. It gives us the warm fuzzies.

We often hear charity being referred to as "giving back." I take exception to this, and I'll tell you why: "Giving back" implies that your wealth was given to you.

I beg to differ. Even if you inherited your wealth, that wealth was still earned. The phrase "giving back" is like a form of self-deprecation. It diminishes the value of what is an undeniably good deed.

Give yourself some credit. You're not "giving back"; you're just giving.

Whether you're paying for your children's or grand-children's education, donating to charities, or helping someone to get a business off the ground, you're still giving. And that's an admirable thing. It gives you a great feeling of joy.

Once we acknowledge that giving—because we enjoy it—isn't entirely selfless, it's easier to see that there isn't anything wrong with structuring our charity in a way that is conducive to successful wealth management. It doesn't make the act any less kind; it doesn't detract from or otherwise tarnish the happiness we're giving others.

It's just smart.

Did you ever stop to think about why charitable donations are tax-deductible? It's because so many of the taxes we pay already go to charity—that's what most government social programs are. We're helping our fellow Americans who can't afford food or housing or medical care. By making charitable donations tax-deductible, the govern-ment allows us to, in effect, choose which charities get our money. We have the opportunity to bypass the bureaucratic waste and fraud that can occur by allowing our government to pick where our tax dollars—at least to the extent of those particular deductions—are going.

It's a win-win. And neither of those wins cancels out the other.

When we travel by air, the flight attendant tells you to put on your own oxygen mask before helping anyone around you put on theirs. (If you're flying with Southwest Airlines, they joke that you should put on your mask first, then help those you *like the most*.) Helping ourselves helps us to help others.

This same concept applies to giving, no matter what form it takes. The more we're able to help ourselves, the more we're able to help others.

It's your money, whether you worked for it, inherited it, or won the lottery. Spend it on the things you want to spend it on. Give it to the causes you care about, help the people you want to help. These are the things *enjoyment* is all about.

And if this enjoyment also helps you to protect, grow, or transfer your wealth?

Another win-win. I tell people to do this all day long.

SECTION IV

Transfer Your Wealth

Creating Your Lasting Legacy

Nobody wants to die. Heck, most of us don't even want to think about death.

For the majority of our lives, our own mortality is pushed to the furthest recesses of our minds, occasionally brought to the forefront by close calls and the sad passing of friends and loved ones. Otherwise, we don't like to talk about it. When we do, we couch the subject in euphemisms like "passed on" or "deceased" or "expired," or even using darkly humorous words and phrases like "croaked" or "kicked the bucket."

I'm no different. As I've mentioned, I sometimes refer to death as "when your will matures." It's this reluctance to ponder our inevitable fates that contributes to so many Americans not even having wills.

Successful wealth management requires us to think about it. More than that, it requires us to prepare for it. This final section of the book may not be as fun as the previous sections (to the extent that any book on wealth management might be construed as "fun"), but it's a topic neglected not at your own peril but at the peril of those you love the most.

IT'S GOTTA GO SOMEWHERE

On the day you die, everything you own—all you've built, all you've accumulated, every single material thing you have as a living, breathing human being—no longer belongs to you. There is no "you," at least not one that retains ownership of a single worldly possession.

It's gotta go somewhere.

Think of your wealth like a river. When you pass away, that river doesn't evaporate; it continues to flow, only now it has to pass through a series of dams, each one stemming that flow. The degree to which each dam holds back the river of your wealth depends on how well you prepared for the inevitable.

This series of dams are the *takers*—those who take their money off the top, whether you would like them to or not. These will include entities like the government, certain businesses and institutions, and even other wealthy people. We'll talk about these takers in the first chapter of this section.

Whatever is left of your river of wealth will then flow to the *getters*—those to whom you want your money to go. These are your heirs and the charities or causes that meant the most to you during your life. We'll discuss these in the final chapter of this section.

A great result, as you may have guessed, ensures that the dam takers (see what I did there? I never said this couldn't be a little bit fun) don't stem the flow of your river by even a drop more than necessary, and that the getters are left with a vigorous stream, rather than a trickle.

Creating a lasting legacy is about securing a future beyond your own. But it's not entirely altruistic. A certain invaluable peace of mind comes from knowing your hard-earned wealth will continue to benefit others long after "your will matures" and you're "pushing up daisies."

16

The Takers

In this chapter we're going to talk about those damned dams (pardon my French). Those entities that—when your will matures—get the first pieces of your estate "pie."

These are the dam takers in order of their share:

THE GOVERNMENT

The government is our first dam taker. Some time ago, a married couple came to see me. The subject of a will came up. Neither of them had one.

"If you were to die today," I asked them, "who do you think would get your assets?"

"Since we're married," the husband said, "I guess all my assets would go to my wife."

"And all my assets would go to my husband," the wife chimed in.

"Okay," I said. "And how about if, tragically, both of you went at the same time?"

They were stumped.

Finally, the husband replied, "To the government?"

There are a lot of folks who believe this. We've lived so long in the era of big government that many Americans default to these types of assumptions.

The good news: It's not quite that bad.

The bad news: It's not entirely wrong.

To borrow a phrase from the Coen brothers' film *Raising Arizona*: "Government do take a bite, don't she?"[5]

She do. There are estate and inheritance taxes (both federal and state), taxes on the money in retirement accounts and investments (and the money those accounts continue to earn after you die), gift taxes, and federal "generation-skipping transfer taxes," to name a few. These will vary significantly based on the state you reside in upon your passing. Some of these taxes will be taken off the top, so to speak; others will become the burden of your heirs.

Whether you have a will or not, the government is going to try to take a bite. Preventing this—which includes estate planning and regularly updated legal documents and beneficiary designations—is about taking the necessary steps to ensure that the bite is more of a nibble (or no snack at all).

FINANCIAL INSTITUTIONS

Financial institutions are our second dam taker. Whether it's a bank, a credit card company, a mutual fund, an annuity, or

---

5   *Raising Arizona*, directed by Joel Coen and Ethan Coen (Los Angeles: Circle Films, 1987).

other type of insurance product, financial institutions have multiple ways of taking a piece of your estate pie after your will matures.

Banks can charge penalties for early withdrawals of funds invested in CDs or to release certain types of accounts. Mutual funds and annuities can charge for closing accounts or can make it difficult to access the accounts quickly. And sometimes it's easier to pay a premium on an insurance policy than to receive a claim. (I hope you sensed my sarcasm there—the former is almost always easier.)

Additionally, any secured loans—such as car loans or your home's mortgage—will have to be paid by your survivors. Your joint credit card accounts will have to be paid by the surviving person on the account as well. Outstanding student loans (and more and more Americans are dying before they've paid off these loans) may—depending on the type of loan—have to be repaid by your estate or the cosigner of the loan. Can you imagine losing a loved one with debt you've signed as a cosigner and getting a statement and payment due every month until that loan is paid off?

Your best financial plan requires not only strategies to avoid some of these pitfalls after you're gone but also strategies to sidestep them while you're still living so that more of your wealth goes exactly where you want it to go when you're gone.

OTHER BUSINESS ENTITIES

Business entities are our third dam taker. A recent article on Debt.org cites two different studies showing that nearly 75 percent of Americans die with some sort of outstanding debt.[6] As you might guess, not all these debts are owed to financial institutions.

We've all seen posted in our local newspapers what's known as a *notice to creditors*, stating that somebody has passed away and giving the creditors a specified period of time to claim what they're owed from the estate. The specific regulations regarding such notices (and how they're disseminated to the creditors) vary state by state, but you can be certain that they will be noticed. Your heirs may find out about debts you owed that you didn't even remember you owed.

These notices are part of the *probate* process, which can itself cost a bundle (even more so if you don't have a will). There are probate attorneys' fees, costs for assessors and appraisers to provide valuation of your assets, costs for newspaper notices and auctions. And all this happens before your heirs start paying off the creditors, at which point they may need attorneys to help them settle some of the larger debts.

And because probate laws also vary state by state, your heirs will need a different probate attorney in each state in which you own real property.

6   "What Happens When People Die with Debt: Who Pays?" 2023. Debt. Org. May 16, 2023. https://www.debt.org/family/people-are-dying-in-debt.

We haven't even talked about medical bills and funeral expenses. Many Americans spend more on health care in the last three months of their lives than in all the rest of their lives combined. Too often, these costs either exceed the insurance coverage or aren't covered at all. You can bet the providers of this care are going to (rightfully) want their money. And—unless you've preplanned and prepaid for your funeral (something few people do, in part for the reasons listed in the opening of this section)—those costs will also be borne by your survivors at a time when they're already undergoing tremendous stress and sorrow.

The probate process is never quick (it can take years in some cases, especially for larger estates), and it's rarely cheap. The right financial strategy while you're still with us can ensure that things go more smoothly (and at less cost) for your loved ones when you're not.

OTHER WEALTHY PEOPLE

Other wealthy people (apart from the most-likely wealthy attorneys and doctors and bankers and such, mentioned above) are the final dam in your river of wealth as it flows to your heirs. I'm referring to those who will be at your estate auction, snatching up your valuable assets at sometimes pennies on the dollar. We've all heard the tales of valuable art and other collectibles being purchased at such auctions for peanuts and later sold at a vast profit—profit that, rightfully, should have gone to your heirs.

Family ignorance creates other's wealth.

With the right knowledge and implementation before your will matures—including ongoing and regularly updated asset valuation—you can make sure that wealth goes into your heirs' pockets instead.

Your best plan isn't just about protecting your money. It's not just about growing or enjoying your money either. It's also about doing all these things with an eye toward not just your future, but the futures of those for whom you've worked so hard to earn what you have.

17

The Getters

You worked hard for most of your life. In your younger years, you worked—whether through college or at your trade or both—to gain the skills you needed to find success in your field. Then you worked to provide for a family and keep a roof over your heads. Then you worked to ensure that you could one day retire and no longer have to work (unless you're one of those who so loves what they do that you never retire).

It's been estimated that, over the course of our lifetimes, we will work around ninety thousand hours. One-third of our lives. In the end, what was it all for?

For most folks, including the majority of my firm's clients, it was for our spouses and children. The loves of our lives.

In the last chapter, we talked about the dam takers— those entities that, without the right financial health strategy, will become our biggest beneficiaries upon our passing. In this chapter we're going to discuss what we need to do— beyond the wealth management strategies to circumvent those dams to the greatest extent possible—in order to ensure that our heirs and beneficiaries are exactly who we want them to be.

BENEFICIARY DESIGNATION

On its face, this may seem like a fairly straightforward concept: We write our will, and we designate who gets what. And that's that. After all, that's what a will is for, right?

In reality, it's far from being that straightforward.

Many—probably most—people believe that their will is the be-all and end-all of beneficiary designation. That the will reigns supreme.

That's nowhere near the truth. It's not just that a huge number of Americans don't regularly update their wills (for those who even have wills). An even more common mistake—and even more perilous for your heirs—is that they don't regularly update the beneficiary designations on assets like life insurance policies, annuities, and IRAs.

Guess what? These designations are the be-all and end-all for those assets. It doesn't matter what your will says.

And guess what else? Many of these beneficiary designations—especially on life insurance policies—are written by amateurs. Sometimes they're written by the life insurance agent whose limited training has been focused primarily on selling policies. Sometimes, especially with policies bought online, they're written by the policyholder themselves. Frequently—and I'm telling you this because I've seen it—the beneficiaries will be written as "spouse" and "children," rather than their actual names. And the insurance companies will accept these.

As I mentioned in chapter 3, our life insurance policies (for many of us) will, upon our deaths, be our greatest transference of wealth. They can also be our greatest transference of wealth to the wrong people.

Let me tell you a sad, but true, story.

Years ago a woman we'll call Sue was referred to me by partners in her husband's law firm. Her husband, Joe, had recently passed away, and Sue needed help straightening out his life insurance. She arrived at my office with a cardboard box full of Joe's multiple policies—policies that amounted to roughly $5.5 million of life insurance proceeds.

After having Sue sign some forms that gave us authorization to contact the various life insurance companies on her behalf, we set about determining the status of the policies.

Here's what we found out:

Of that $5.5 million in life insurance, $2 million of the policies had been cancelled for years. Joe had either let them lapse or had cancelled them himself. Now that $5.5 million becomes $3.5 million. Another $500,000 went to cover loans Joe had made on the policies. Now we're at $3 million. What a terrible result.

But wait. It gets worse.

Sue had been Joe's third wife, and they had been together long enough to have two kids and see them reach middle and high school, respectively. Joe also had two children from his first wife, but they were both grown, had graduated college, and were thriving. His younger kids and his widow, however, still needed support. More than the day-to-day necessities; college was on the horizon. While Sue was understandably disheartened by the $2.5 million hit that box of policies had taken, she knew that $3 million would at least make the necessities, and college for the kids, less of a burden.

A third of what remained—$1 million—was left to Joe's first wife. Whether this was intentional or not, no one would ever know. My feeling, and Sue's, was that it was negligence on Joe's part. Remember: Life insurance companies can't legally alter the beneficiaries on a policy; only the policyholder can.

As the bearer of bad news, I had to watch, with each tragic update, Sue's hopes for the future crumble before her eyes.

And the hits just kept on coming.

Another $800,000 went to Joe's second wife. At one point Sue thought she had $5.5 million. Now she had $1.2 million. And I can assure you, neither of Joe's ex-wives were giving Sue back any of *their* money.

Most financial experts will tell you that if you begin your retirement with $1.2 million, you can expect to live on about 4 percent of that ($48,000) annually and not run out of money during your lifetime. For Sue, that meant raising two teenagers and putting them through college on about a third of what Joe had been earning per year as an attorney.

It was devastating for Sue. And I've no doubt it would have been the last thing Joe wanted.

Had these life insurance policies been IRAs or annuities, the results would have been exactly the same.

By all means, have a will. Make it specific. Update it regularly. But don't neglect your beneficiary designations. Your life insurance policies and other financial accounts will be far more important.

CHARITIES

For most of us, charity begins at home. It's where—when our wills mature—we want our money to go after the family is taken care of. There are also those who don't have much family to speak of. Maybe most of their family is already gone. Maybe they never had children. Maybe they want their kids to fend for themselves, like they had to do. It's fairly rare, but not unheard of.

In chapter 15 we talked about charitable giving while you're still among us. Let's briefly discuss giving when we're gone.

You can, of course, leave money or other assets to charity in your will. You can also leave money directly to charity via your beneficiary designations. Or you can create what's known as a *charitable gift annuity*, whereby you contract with the specific charity (rather than an insurance company) to receive the financial benefits of the annuity while you're still living (creating a tax break), and after you pass away the remainder transfers to the charity. Then there are vehicles such as charitable trusts, gift funds, and foundations, to name a few ways that you can coordinate planning your social capital so that you can leave significance beyond your family.

However you choose to do it, you're helping more than the particular charity—you can also benefit your family by lowering the value of your entire estate below the threshold that will subject your heirs to often substantial (in my opinion, *too* substantial) federal and state estate taxes.

Nobody wants to die. But we all do. Successful wealth management requires that we integrate this inevitability into the big picture of our lives—that we realize that protecting, growing, enjoying, and transferring our wealth are all parts of the same puzzle and that every single puzzle is different for every single person.

Ninety-nine percent of financial advisors or wealth managers or gurus or whatever they call themselves won't tell you that.

I will.

I just did.

CONCLUSION
Wealth Management:
A Family Affair

Throughout these pages, I've done my best to convey to you my firmly held belief—based on my decades of experience as a full financial fiduciary—that wealth management is much more than stocks and bonds and various other investments. It's more than insurance and retirement plans. It's more than ensuring that you don't run out of money before you run out of life and securing the financial security of those you hold most dear when you do. It is about all these things, of course, but no single one of them comes close to being the "whole package." The big picture.

Successful wealth management incorporates all these various elements into strategies that keep their eye on a single perpetual prize: the financial health, well-being, and, with it, the happiness of you and those you love. Not just now, but in a future you won't be around for and for generations to come.

Protect. Grow. *Enjoy.* Transfer. That's what wealth management is supposed to be about. And it's generational. It's a family affair.

Yet, as important as wealth management is to the lives of those you love, I've found that—far too often—money matters are taboo in family discussions. If Social Security and Medicare are supposedly a "third rail" in politics, so it is with candid conversations about finances with the very people most affected by our decisions.

This shouldn't be. We have to get over that.

I can't tell you how many times I've seen families fractured, sometimes irrevocably, over feuds that erupted over financial disputes that arose following the death of a beloved patriarch or matriarch. Bonds forged over a lifetime broken by discord over the dispensation of an estate—sometimes because the deceased didn't plan, sometimes because those left behind didn't know. This only exacerbates an already overwhelming grief, adds fuel to a fire that never should have started in the first place.

My guess is that you've seen this too. Many of you may have experienced it.

Communication is key, and financial health and well-being are too crucial to remain taboo.

Such communication shouldn't begin at retirement or be limited to matters of estate planning. The earlier you begin, the better. Once your children are old enough to understand work and wages and budgets, bring them in on the conversation.

It's this focus on not just wealth management but generational wealth management that distinguishes my firm from most in the industry.

It's what makes me a full financial fiduciary.

I first started working with Gary Johnson in 1997. A couple of years later, he introduced me to his son, Gary Jr., who was thirty-five at the time. Since then, I've worked with all four of Gary's children—and even some of his grand-children. (There's a great-grandchild now, but since he's only five years old, I've not yet started working with him. But I hope to.) As Gary Sr. aged, Gary Jr. began to attend Dad's meetings. This helped Gary Sr. make sure he was still making the correct decisions. When Gary Sr. passed, Gary Jr. handled the estate affairs for the whole family. Sadly, in 2020 Gary Jr. was diagnosed with cancer and passed away in late 2021. We now advise his wife and children.

In a 2014 article in the *Maryland Daily Record* titled, "Wealth Advisers 'not just for the uber-rich,'" Gary said (referring to my company, Raskin Global), "They look at the whole picture, things I don't know about or have an interest in learning about." Later in that same article, he added, "The bottom line is, the Johnson family and heirs are all being comfortably taken care of by somebody who knows what he's doing."[7]

And Gary was right: That *is* the bottom line.

Just a few short weeks ago, I was in Steamboat Springs, Colorado, at the wedding of the oldest daughter of a client I started working with twenty-five years ago. The bride was only ten when I started working with her father. She, too, has been a client of mine for a few years now. As are both of his other children.

I hope I'm around to help *their* children.

I've never believed that money is the key to happiness. But stress over money can be (and often is) a source of despair. My job is to help you find happiness by eliminating that despair.

Wealth management done properly—with the correct focus on *protecting, growing,* and *enjoying* your wealth now and *transferring* it when you're gone—is what it's all about.

---

7   Pete Pichaske. 2014. "Wealth Advisers 'Not Just for the Uber-Rich.'" *Maryland Daily Record*, September 12, 2014. https://thedailyrecord.com/2014/09/12/wealth-advisers-not-just-for-the-uber-rich/.

ABOUT THE AUTHOR

Like you, personal finance specialist and noted media contributor Leonard Raskin has seen significant change in money matters and management during his career of over thirty-six years. How does he help you deal with these changes? Is it by suggesting the best stocks and bonds? Is it by advising on asset allocation and location strategies? Is it by helping you choose the correct disability or life insurance products? Or is it an overall view of you living a financially balanced life?

Yes. It's all these things, and more.

The financial markets are crowded with advice and products, along with companies that make questionable promises about attaining your financial goals. Leonard's approach is radically different. Through his unique process of education, state-of-the-art technology, and an unwavering philosophy, he can help you navigate the financial marketplace. He can achieve the seemingly impossible task of breaking through the clutter by helping you to understand what's in your best interest.

Leonard has a unique ability to simplify the complexities of an ever-evolving financial marketplace. His fusion of straightforward, honest advice with a warm personal touch is what you can expect from the team at Raskin Global.

Leonard holds a master's degree in financial services, is a CFP™, ChFC, CLU, CASL,* CAP, and AEP, and works with multiple charitable organizations and foundations. This education and experience, along with Leonard's friendly and welcoming demeanor, instill confidence in his clients. When it comes to matters of long-term financial health, Leonard's clients know they're in capable and caring hands.

Born and raised in Baltimore, Leonard now lives in Phoenix, Maryland, twenty minutes from his childhood home. Married for nearly thirty years to Kathy (Uhlan), a certified public accountant, they have a son in college and a dog at home.

*The Chartered Advisor for Senior Living® (CASL®) designation is issued by The American College of Financial Services.

www.ingramcontent.com/pod-product-compliance
Lightning Source LLC
Chambersburg PA
CBHW021458180326
41458CB00051B/6870/J